ABOUT KUMON

MATH. READING. SUCCESS.

What is Kumon?

Kumon is the world's largest supplemental education provider and a leader in producing outstanding results. After-school programs in math and reading at Kumon Centers around the globe have been helping children succeed for 50 years.

Kumon Workbooks represent just a fraction of our complete curriculum of preschool-to-college-level material assigned at Kumon Centers under the supervision of trained Kumon Instructors.

The Kumon Method enables each child to progress successfully by practicing material until concepts are mastered and advancing in small, manageable increments. Instructors carefully assign materials and pace advancement according to the strengths and needs of each individual student.

Students usually attend a Kumon Center twice a week and practice at home the other five days. Assignments take about twenty minutes.

Kumon helps students of all ages and abilities master the basics, improve concentration and study habits, and build confidence.

How did Kumon begin?

IT ALL BEGAN IN JAPAN 50 YEARS AGO when a parent and teacher named Toru Kumon found a way to help his son Takeshi do better in school. At the prompting of his wife, he created a series of short assignments that his son could complete successfully in less than 20 minutes a day and that would ultimately make high school math easy. Because each was just a bit more challenging than the last, Takeshi was able to master the skills and gain the confidence to keep advancing.

This unique self-learning method was so successful that Toru's son was able to do calculus by the time he was in the sixth grade. Understanding the value of good reading comprehension, Mr. Kumon then developed a reading program employing the same method. His programs are the basis and inspiration of those offered at Kumon Centers today under the expert guidance of professional Kumon Instructors.

Mr. Toru Kumon
Founder of Kumon

What can Kumon do for my child?

Kumon is geared to children of all ages and skill levels. Whether you want to give your child a leg up in his or her schooling, build a strong foundation for future studies or address a possible learning problem, Kumon provides an effective program for developing key learning skills given the strengths and needs of each individual child.

What makes Kumon so different?

Kumon uses neither a classroom model nor a tutoring approach. It's designed to facilitate self-acquisition of the skills and study habits needed to improve academic performance. This empowers children to succeed on their own, giving them a sense of accomplishment that fosters further achievement. Whether for remedial work or enrichment, a child advances according to individual ability and initiative to reach his or her full potential. Kumon is not only effective, but also surprisingly affordable.

What is the role of the Kumon Instructor?

Kumon Instructors regard themselves more as mentors or coaches than teachers in the traditional sense. Their principal role is to provide the direction, support and encouragement that will guide the student to performing at 100% of his or her potential. Along with their rigorous training in the Kumon Method, all Kumon Instructors share a passion for education and an earnest desire to help children succeed.

KUMON FOSTERS:

- A mastery of the basics of reading and math
- Improved concentration and study habits
- Increased self-discipline and self-confidence
- A proficiency in material at every level
- Performance to each student's full potential
- A sense of accomplishment

▶▶ GETTING STARTED IS EASY. Just call us at 877.586.6671 or visit kumon.com to request our free brochure and find a Kumon Center near you. We'll direct you to an Instructor who will be happy to speak with you about how Kumon can address your child's particular needs and arrange a free placement test. There are more than 1,700 Kumon Centers in the U.S. and Canada, and students may enroll at any time throughout the year, even summer. Contact us today.

FIND OUT MORE ABOUT KUMON MATH & READING CENTERS.
Receive a free copy of our parent guide, *Every Child an Achiever*, by visiting kumon.com/go.survey or calling **877.586.6671**

 Cherries

example

To parents:
Your child will practice filling in white areas in the following illustrations. It's okay if your child can't color the entire white spot neatly, and don't be concerned if he or she colors outside of the lines.

✳ Color the white area below.

 red

To parents:
This page will provide your child with practice drawing lines. Have your child draw a line from the dot to the star, avoiding the obstacles along the way.

✻ Using a red crayon, draw a line from the dot (●) to the star (★) without touching any cherries.

2 Grapes

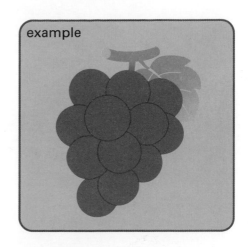

example

✳ Color the white area below.

violet

✱ Using a **violet (purple)** crayon, draw a line from the dot (●) to the star (★) without touching any grapes.

3 Bananas

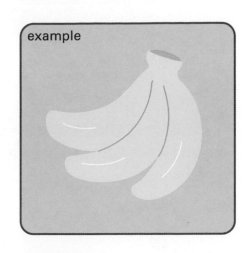

example

✳ Color the white area below.

 yellow

※ Using a **yellow** crayon, draw a line from the dot (●) to the star (★) without touching any bananas.

4 Watermelon

✳ Color the white area below.

green

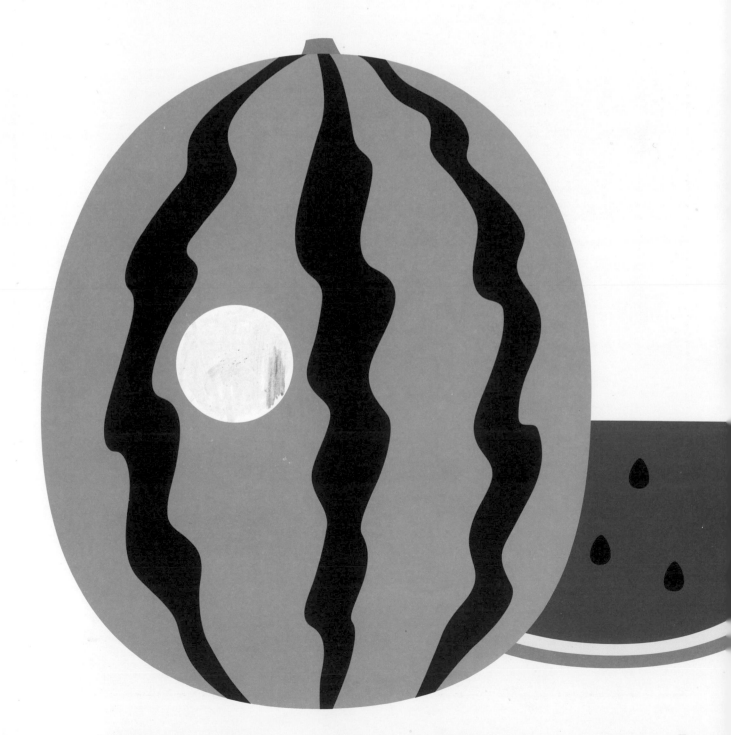

✳ Using a **green** crayon, draw a line from the dot (●) to the star (★) without touching any watermelons.

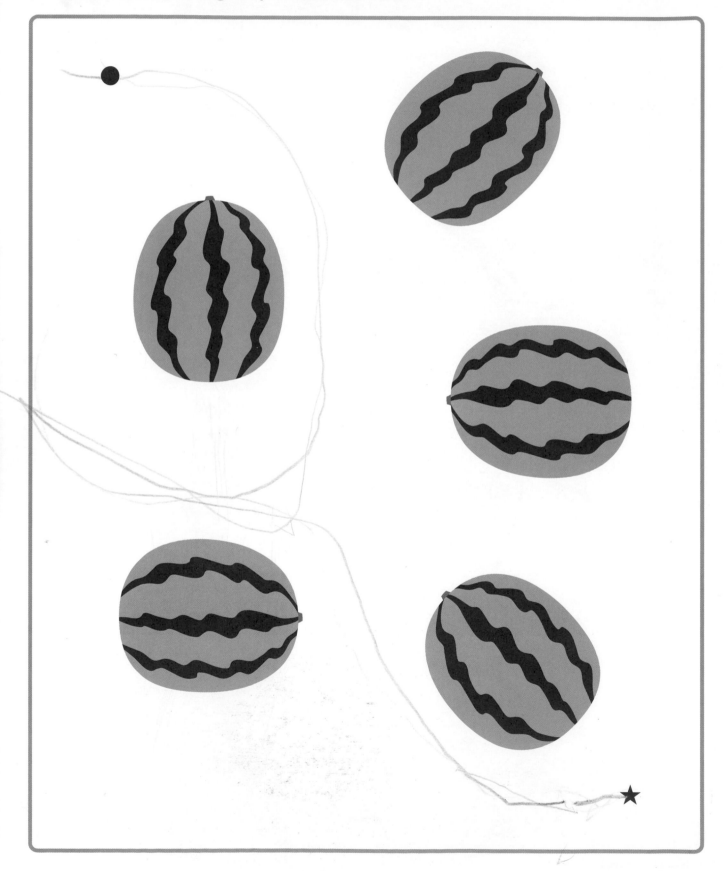

5 Tomatoes

✱ Color the white area below.

red

✱ Using a **red** crayon, draw a line from the dot (●) to the star (★) without touching any tomatoes.

 # Carrots

✳ Color the white area below. orange

11

✳ Using an **orange** crayon, draw a line from the dot (●) to the
star (★) without touching any carrots.

7 Cheese

example

✱ Color the white area below.

yellow

✳ Using a **yellow** crayon, draw a line from the dot (●) to the star (★) without touching any cheese.

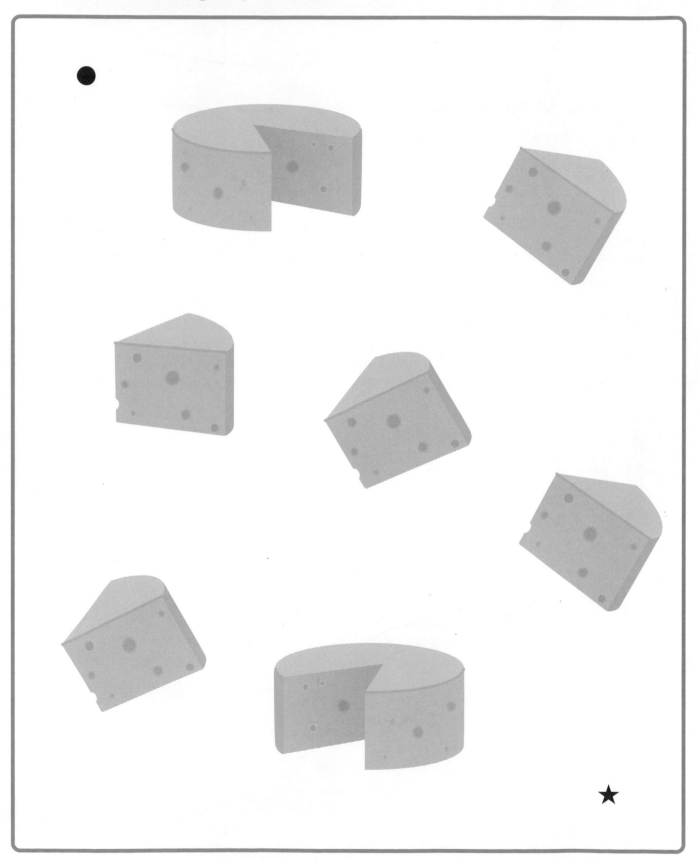

8 Hamburger

example

✱ Color the white area below.

brown

Using a **brown** crayon, draw a line from the dot (●) to the star (★) without touching any hamburgers.

9 Spaghetti

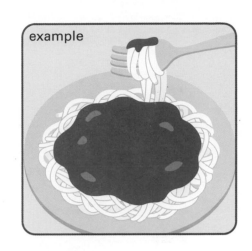
example

✳ Color the white area below.

 red

✸ Using a **red** crayon, draw a line from the dot (●) to the star (★) without touching any spaghetti.

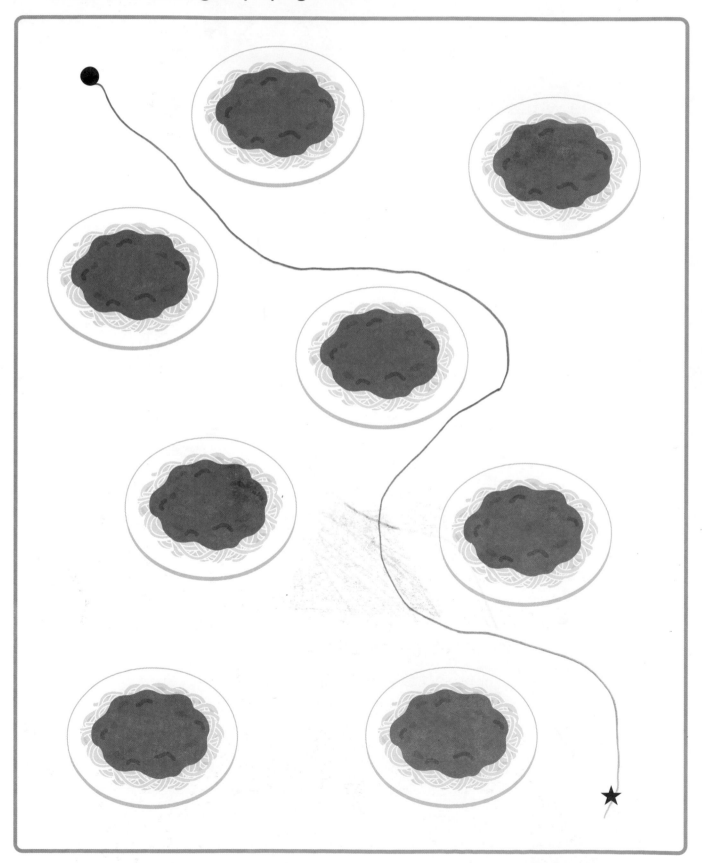

10 Police Car

example

* Color the white area below.

black

✳ Using a **black** crayon, draw a line from the dot (●) to the star (★) without touching any police cars.

11 School Bus

example

✱ Color the white area below.

yellow

✱ Using a **yellow** crayon, draw a line from the dot (●) to the star (★) without touching any school buses.

 **Fire Engine**

example

✱ Color the white area below. red

✳ Using a **red** crayon, draw a line from the dot (●) to the star (★) without touching any fire engines.

24

 **Whale**

To parents:
The white area is now larger. Offer praise
when your child is done coloring.

example

✱ Color the white area below.

 black

✳ Using a **black** crayon, draw a line from the dot (●) to the star (★) without touching any whales.

14 Dog

example

* Color the white area below.

brown

27

※ Using a **brown** crayon, draw a line from the dot (●) to the star (★) without touching any dogs.

Panda

example

✴ Color the white area below.

black

✳ Using a **black** crayon, draw a line from the dot (●) to the star (★) without touching any pandas.

16 Parrot

✳ Color the white areas below.

example

 blue orange

✳ Using a **blue** crayon, draw a line from the dot (●) to the star (★) without touching any parrots.

Kites

✳ Color the white areas below.

violet   green

33

✱ Using a **violet (purple)** crayon, draw a line from the dot (●) to the star (★) without touching any kites.

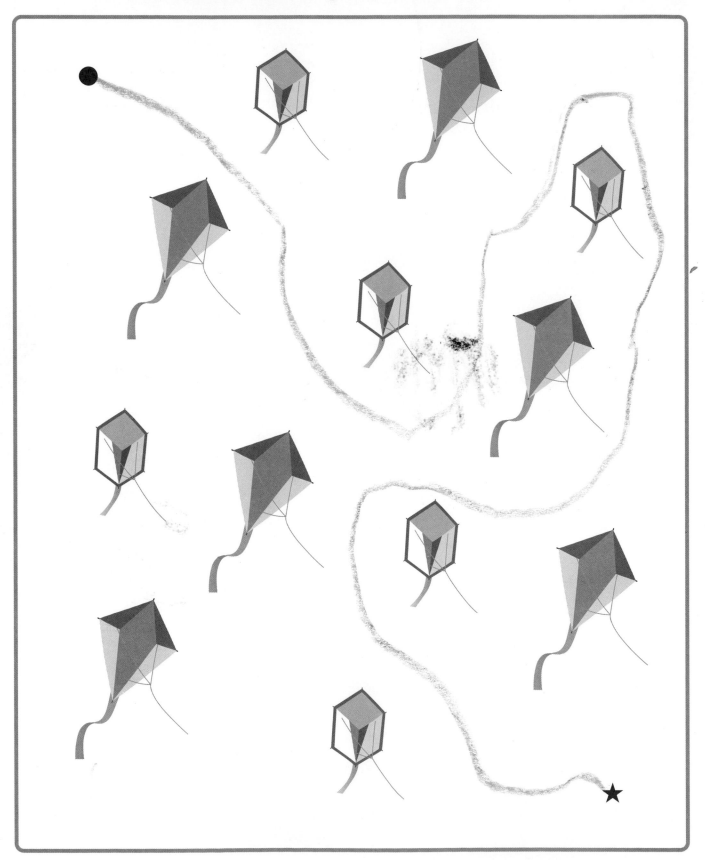

18 Hot Air Balloons

example

✳ Color the white areas below.

brown blue

✳ Using a **blue** crayon, draw a line from the dot (●) to the star (★) without touching any hot air balloons.

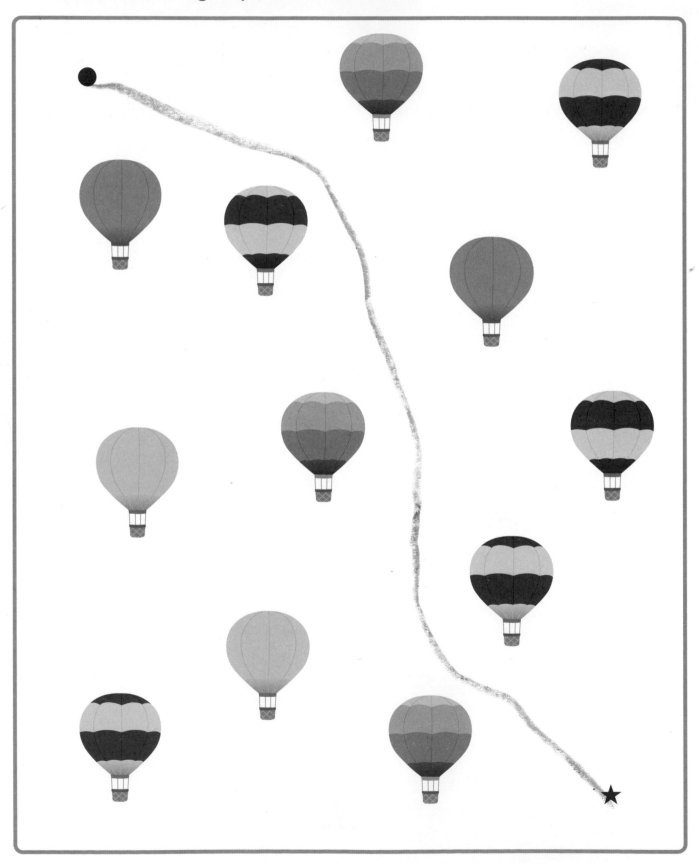

19 Beach Umbrellas

example

✳ Color the white areas below.

 orange blue green

37

* Using an **orange** crayon, draw a line from the dot (●) to the star (★) without touching any beach umbrellas.

20 Tulips

example

✹ **Color the white areas below.**

✳ Using a **green** crayon, draw a line from the dot (●) to the star (★) without touching any tulips.

 Roses

To parents:
From this page on, each exercise will require more careful coloring. It doesn't matter if your child can't color perfectly inside the lines.

✳ Color the rose.

 red

✳ Using a **red** crayon, draw a line from the dot (●) to the star (★) without touching any roses.

22 Sunflower

example

✳ Color the sunflower.

yellow

✳ Using a **yellow** crayon, draw a line from the dot (●) to the star (★) without touching any sunflowers.

23 Butterflies

example

✱ **Color the butterfly.** blue

✱ Using a **blue** crayon, draw a line from the dot (●) to the star (★) without touching any butterflies.

 # Cow

✱ **Color the cow.**

black

✳ Using a **black** crayon, draw a line from the dot (●) to the star (★) without touching any cows.

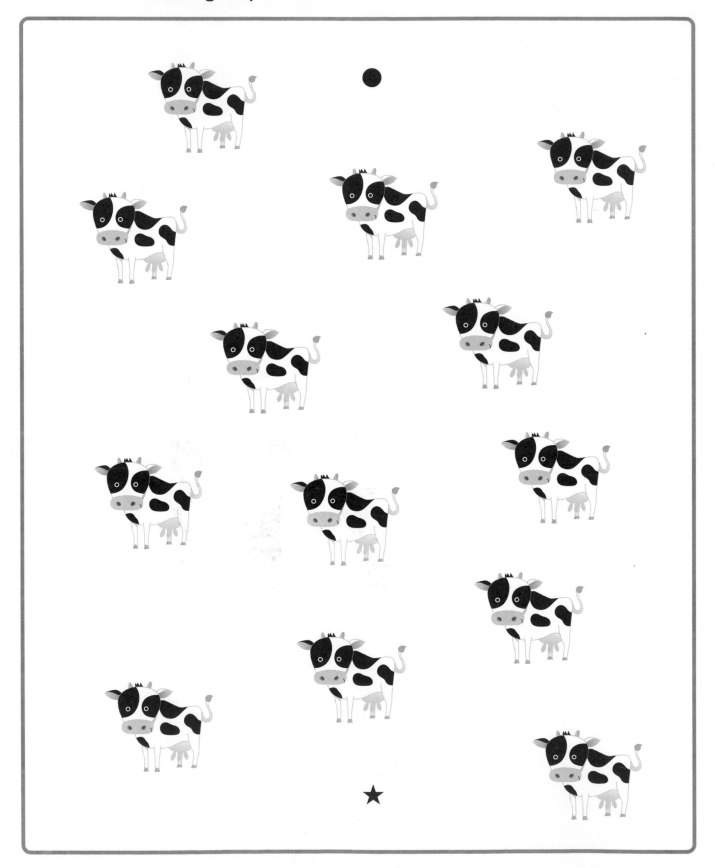

25 Tiger

✳ Color the tiger.

 orange black

49

✳ Using an **orange** crayon, draw a line from the dot (●) to the star
(★) without touching any tigers.

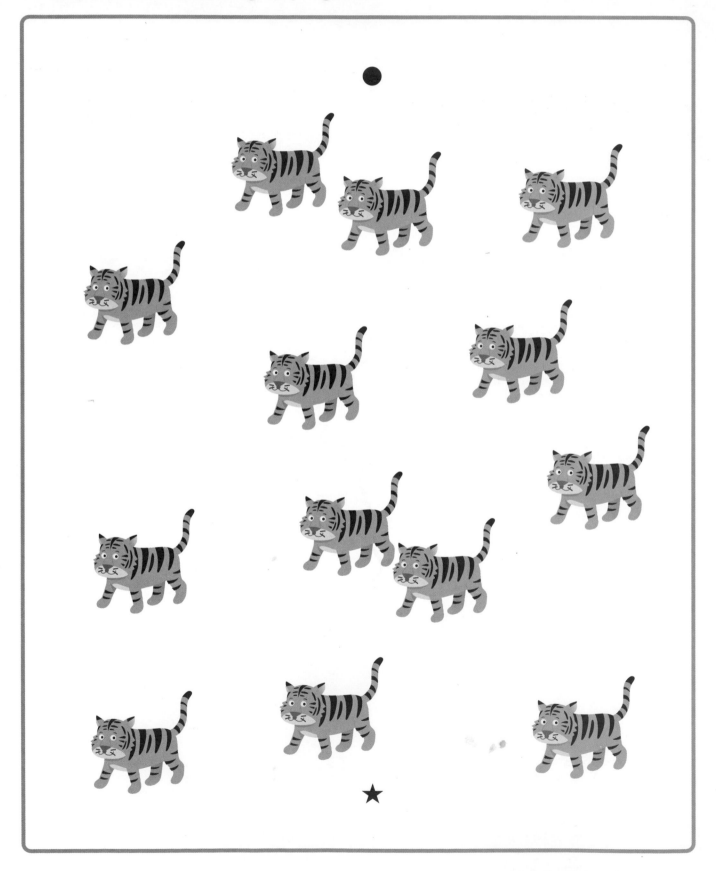

26 Giraffe

example

✳ **Color the giraffe.**

 yellow   brown

51

✳ Using a **brown** crayon, draw a line from the dot (●) to the star (★) without touching any giraffes.

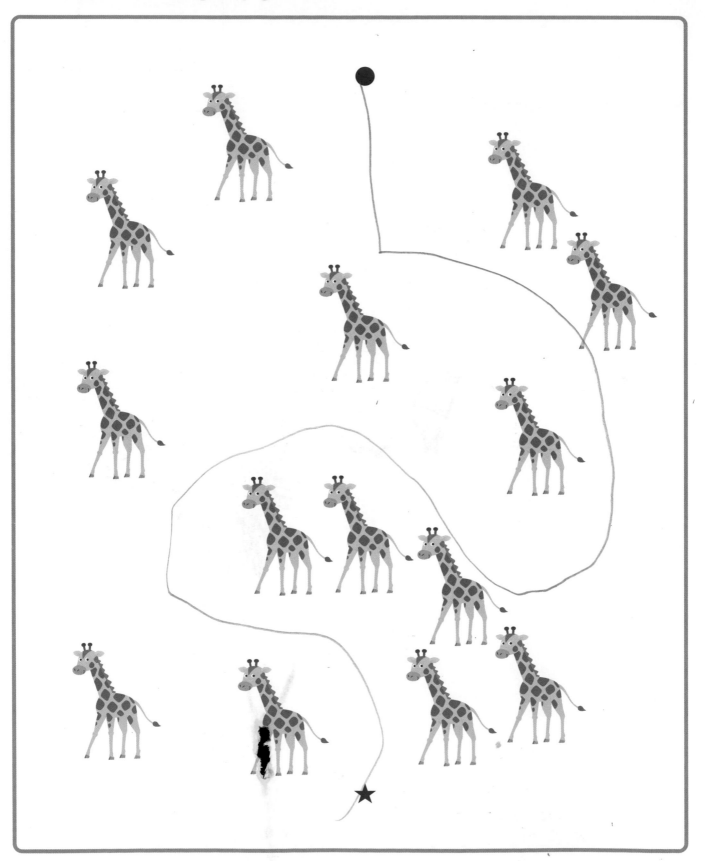

27 Penguin

example

✳ Color the penguin.

yellow orange

53

✳ Using a yellow crayon, draw a line from the dot (●) to the star (★) without touching any penguins.

Traffic Light

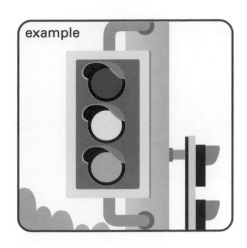

✳ Color the traffic light.

 red green

✳ Using a **green** crayon, draw a line from the dot (●) to the star (★) without touching any traffic lights.

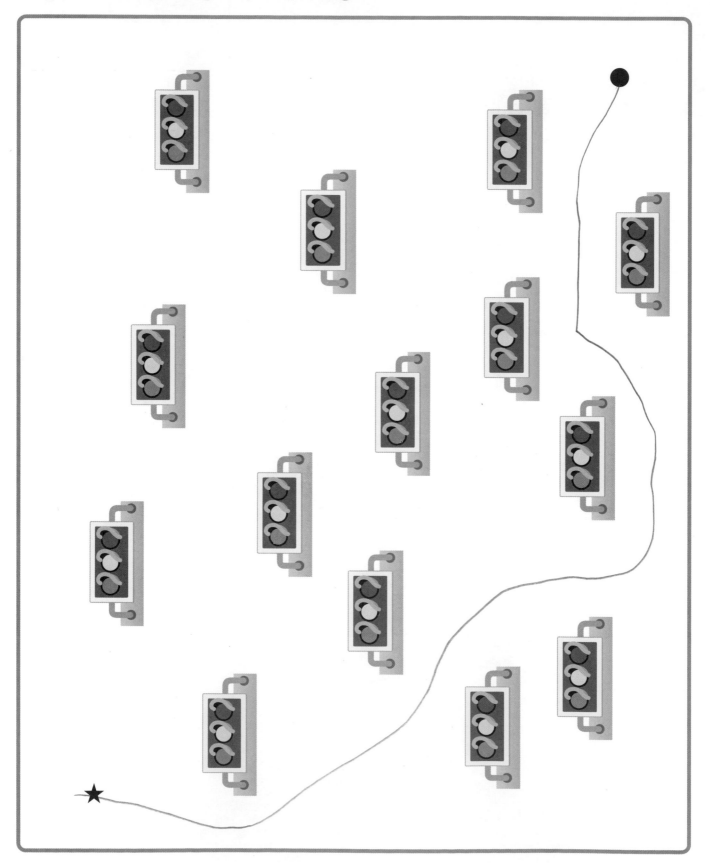

**29** Ice Cream

example

✽ Color the ice cream.

orange   violet

57

✳ Using a **violet (purple)** crayon, draw a line from the dot (●) to the star (★) without touching any ice creams.

30 Cake

example

* Color the cake.

red   yellow   blue

✳ Using a **red** crayon, draw a line from the dot (●) to the star (★) without touching any cakes.

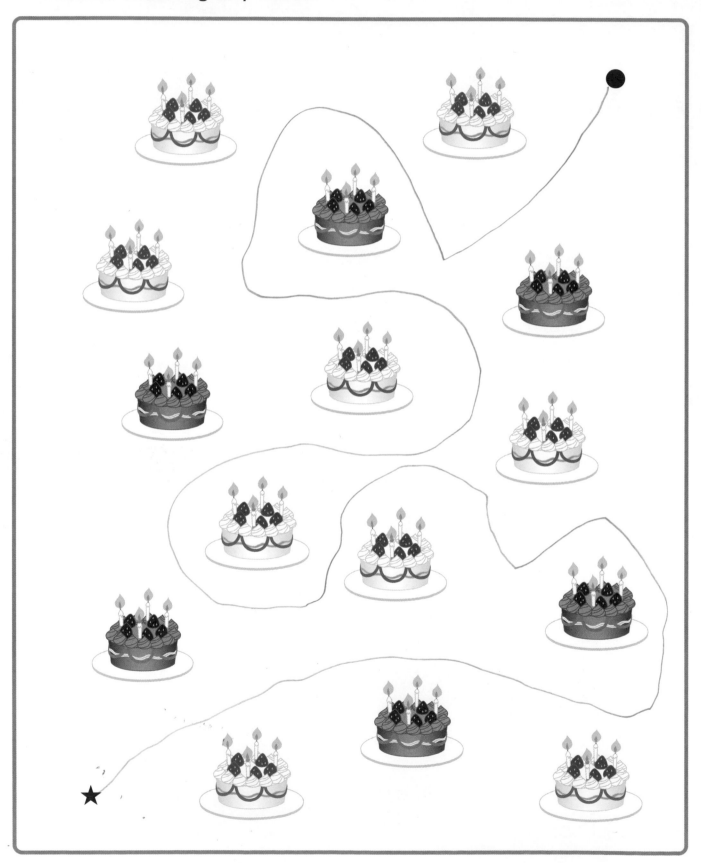

31 Candy

example

✳ Color the candy.

61

✳ Using a **green** crayon, draw a line from the dot (●) to the star (★) without touching any candy.

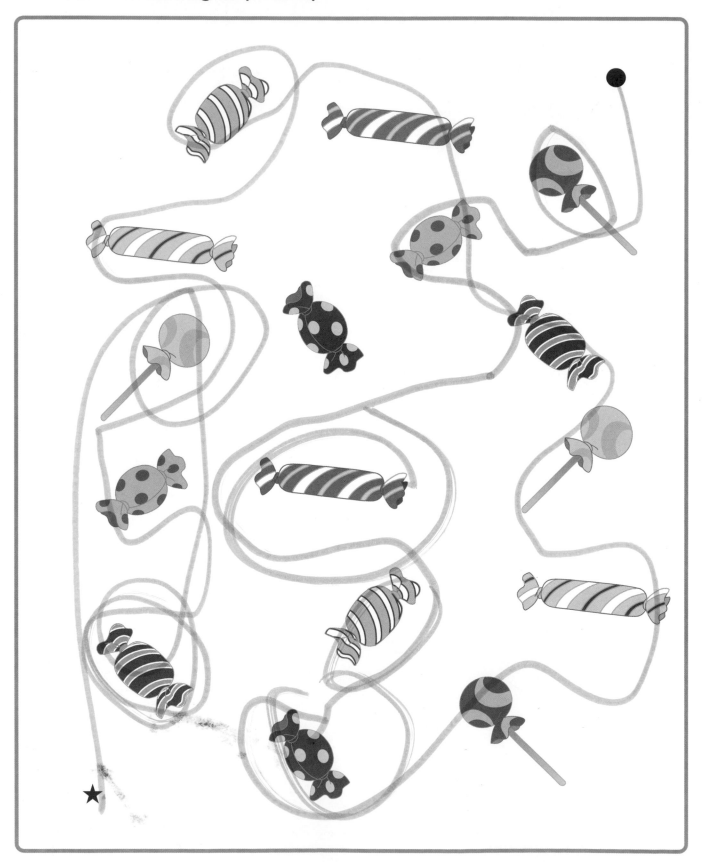

32 Jungle Gym

example

✱ Color the jungle gym.

 red  blue green

✳ Using a **green** crayon, draw a line from the dot (●) to the star (★) without touching any jungle gyms.

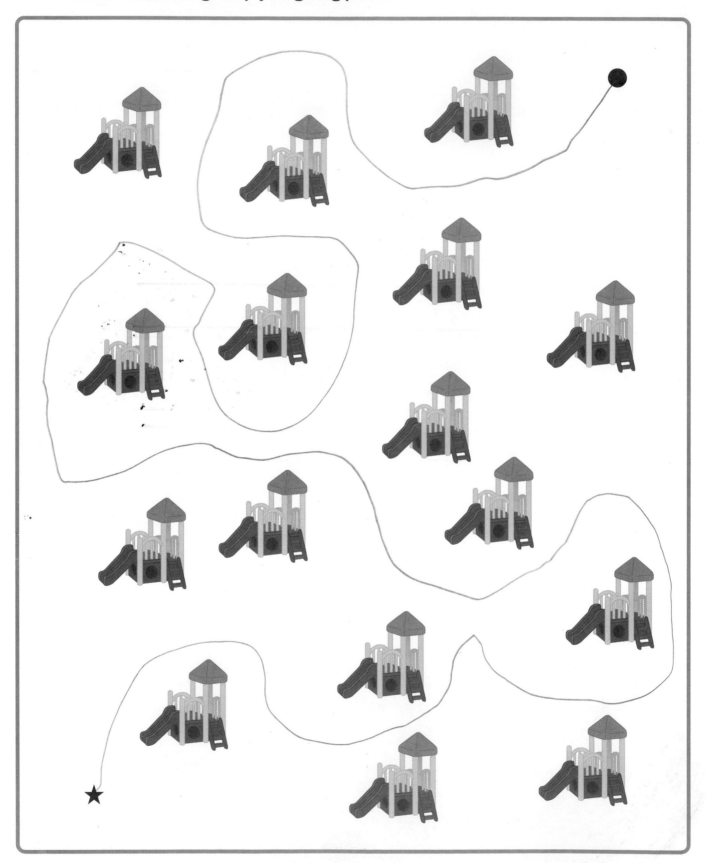

Building Blocks

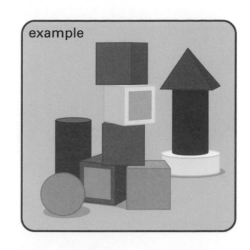

example

✱ Color the blocks.

 brown violet green orange

65

✱ Using a **violet (purple)** crayon, draw a line from the dot (●) to the star (★) without touching any building blocks.

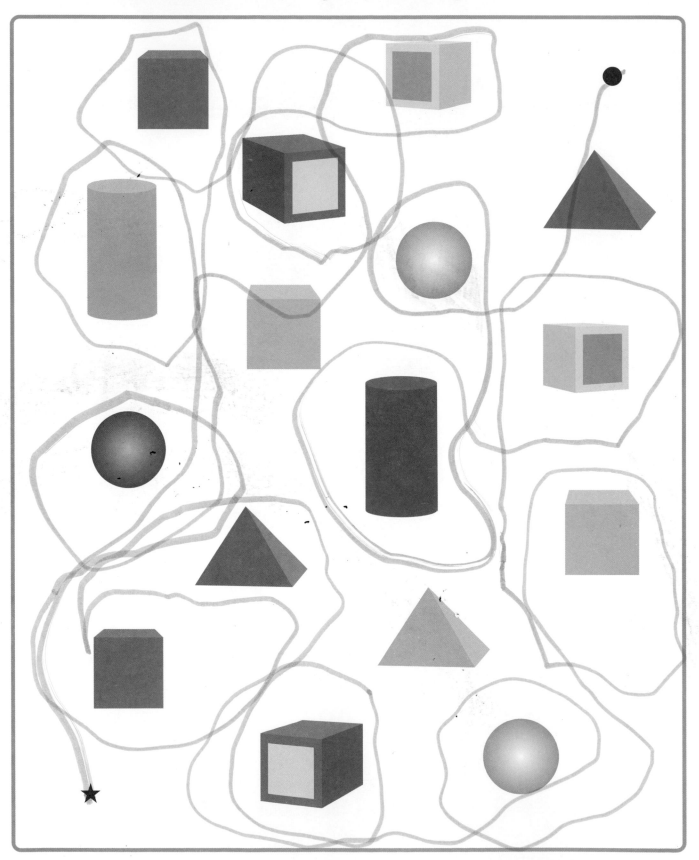

34 Rainbow

example

✳ Color the rainbow.

 blue violet red orange

Using an **orange** crayon, draw a line from the dot (●) to the star (★) without touching any rainbows.

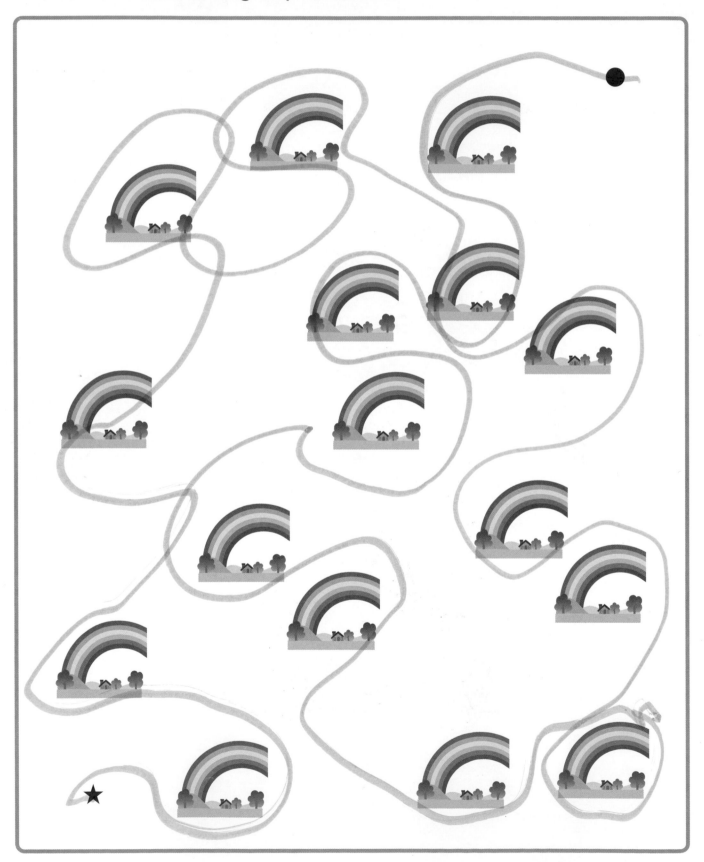

35 Robot

To parents:
From this page on, have your child choose any combination
of colors he or she likes. It's also okay to use a single color.
Let your child be creative.

example

✸ Color the robot with your favorite colors.

✷ Using **your favorite color**, draw a line from the dot (●) to the star (★) without touching any robots.

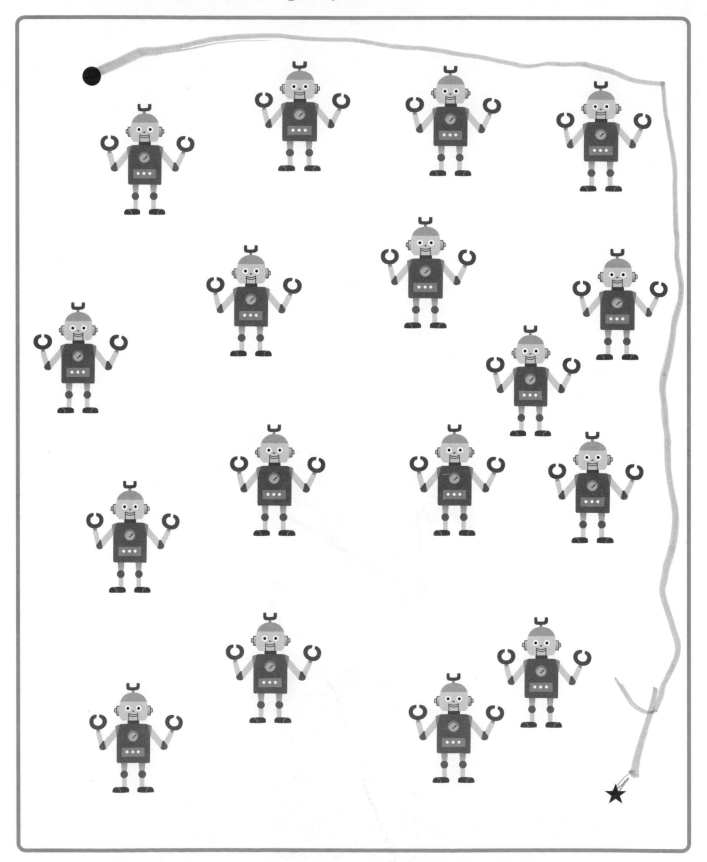

36 Magician

example

✳ Color the magician with your favorite colors.

71

✳ Using **your favorite color**, draw a line from the dot (●) to the star (★) without touching any magicians.

example

* Color the tropical fish with your favorite colors.

✱ Using **your favorite color**, draw a line from the dot (●) to the
star (★) without touching any tropical fish.

 **Present**

example

✳ Color the ribbon with your favorite colors.

✱ Using **your favorite color**, draw a line from the dot (●) to the
star (★) without touching any presents.

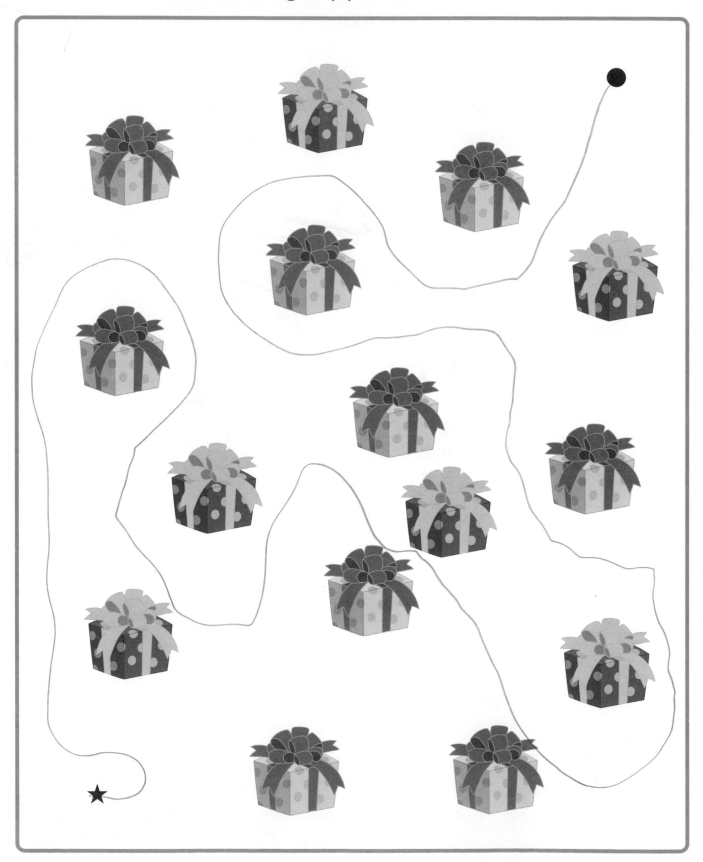

39 Halloween

example

✱ Color the costumes with your favorite colors.

✱ Using **your favorite color**, draw a line from the dot (●) to the
star (★) without touching any trick-or-treaters.

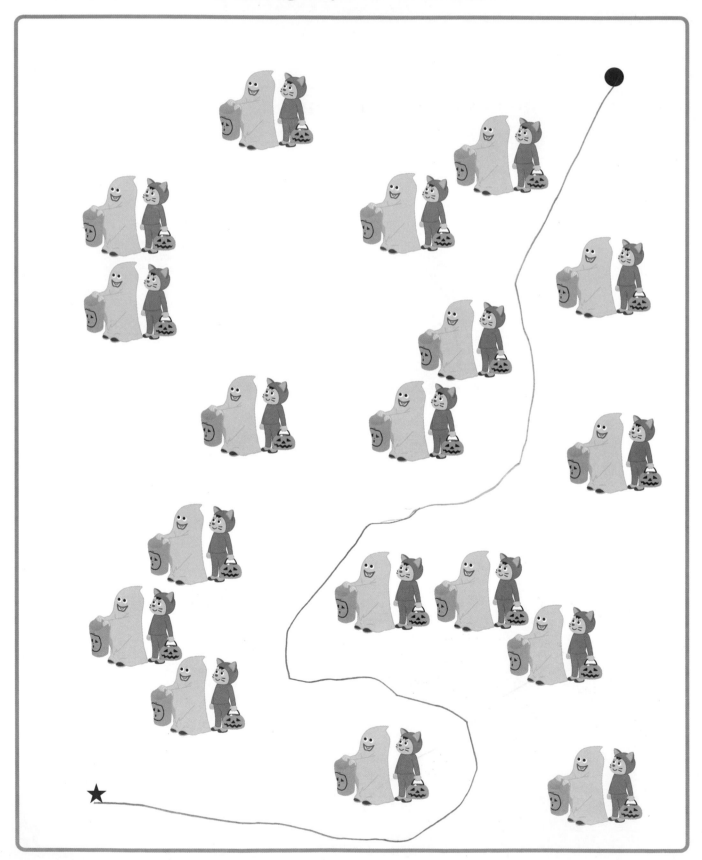

40 Dolls

example

To parents:
This is the last exercise of the book. When your child is finished, compare this page with his or her previous work. You will see significant progress in your child's ability to control the crayon, choose the correct colors, and color evenly. Praise your child for his or her progress.

✳ Color the dolls' clothes with your favorite colors.

✳ Using your favorite color, draw a line from the dot (●) to the star (★) without touching any dolls.

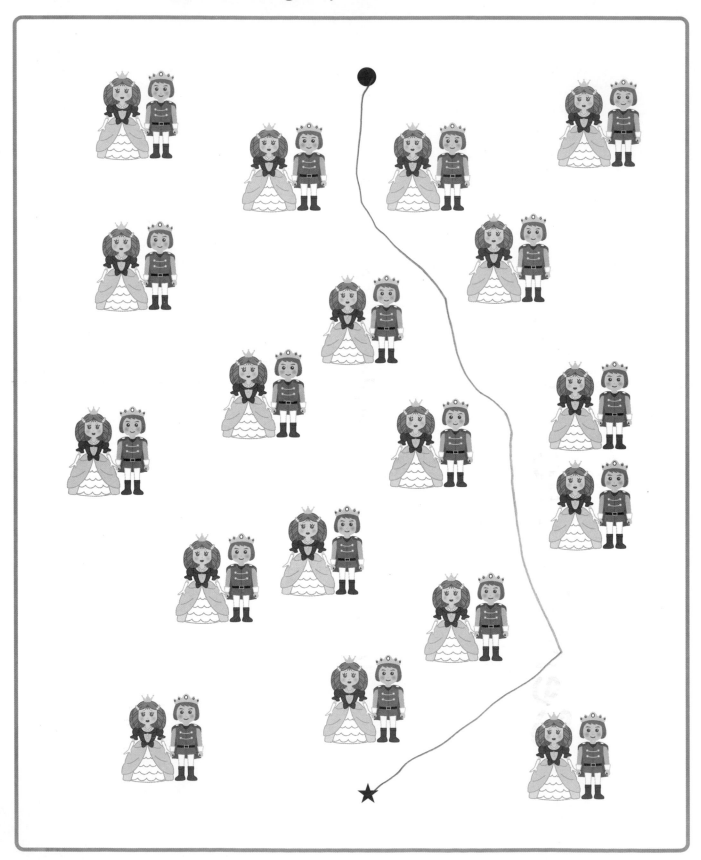

KUMON

Certificate of Achievement

is hereby congratulated on completing

My Book of Coloring

Presented on _____ , 20____

_____
Parent or Guardian